INTRODUCTION

This book contains 60 stencil designs with which you can create greeting cards for more than a dozen holidays and special occasions. Whether you need a large batch of Christmas cards, a small group of birthday invitations or one special valentine, you can undoubtedly find the right subject in this varied collection. Choices include Easter tulips and bunnies, St. Patrick's Day shamrocks and leprechauns, a New Year's bottle of champagne, an umbrella to celebrate a shower and bells to celebrate a wedding.

These stencils can be cut out and used again and again. If you are using marking pens, simply remove the pattern from the book, cut out the black shapes with a stencil knife, center and tape the stencil to your card and color through the open spaces. Each design is centered within four corner brackets to help you align the stencil in the middle of your card. When you are finished coloring, remove the tape and touch up the design if necessary. The designs can be colored through either side; that is, they can be reversed. The illustrations on the covers give examples of attractive color patterns for cards.

The stencils can, of course, also be used for decorating walls, floors, furniture, fabrics, tin, leather and almost any other surface. Complete instructions and a list of materials needed for stenciling with paint and more detailed directions for stenciling on paper are given below. All necessary materials are inexpensive and easy to find in most well-stocked hardware or art-supply stores. The method is easily mastered and projects quickly completed.

LIST OF MATERIALS

boiled linseed oil
turpentine
rags
stencil knife and blades
knife sharpener or carborundum stone
large knitting needles or ice pick
cutting surface (glass, wood, etc.)
masking tape
paint

textile paint (for fabric)
stenciling brushes
newspaper
fine sandpaper
desk blotters (for fabric)
varnish (for floors, wood, tin)
#4 artists' brush
spray fixative (for paper)
colored pencils (for paper)
marking pens (for paper)
sponge (for paper)

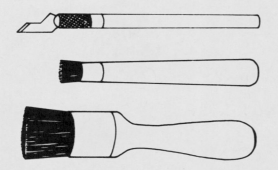

Stencil knife and two stenciling brushes of different sizes.

First, cut out an entire page (= stencil plate) from the book with a pair of scissors. When more than one design appears on a page, a dotted line serves as the cutting guideline for separating each design onto a distinct stencil plate. The margin of ¾ inch or more around the design makes the stencil sturdy and durable while in use and protects the surrounding areas from paint when stenciling.

The pages of this book are of medium-weight manila paper, which must be treated with oil to make it tough, leathery and impervious to moisture. Oiled manila will become semi-translucent, allowing light to penetrate slightly. A knife blade will cut through an oil plate more easily. The oiling process takes place after the plate (page) is cut from the book but before the blacked-in areas of the design are cut out, so there will be no chance of bending or ripping delicate ties (bridge areas) when applying the oil.

A mixture of 50% *boiled* linseed oil and 50% turpentine is applied with a rag to both sides of the plate until it is thoroughly saturated. Using a thumbtack, the plate is then hung to dry. It will dry to touch in about 10 minutes. Any excess can be wiped off with a dry rag or the plate can be allowed to dry for a longer period. The rag should then be immersed in water until it can be incinerated or removed by regular garbage disposal service. Spontaneous combustion can occur if the rag is stored for later use.

The stencil knife is used for cutting out the small pieces through which the paint will reach the surface to be decorated. Only the solid black areas of each design are cut out. Suitable cutting surfaces for this task are hard wood, a piece of plate glass with the edges taped, or a stack of old newspapers. The oiled stencil plate is placed on the cutting surface and allowed to move freely. Grasp the stencil knife as you would a pencil. Apply even pressure for the entire length of a curve or line. Frequent lifting of the knife causes jagged, uneven edges. The small details of the stencil design are cut out first and larger areas last to prevent weakening the plate before cutting is completed. Sharpen the blade frequently on a carborundum stone or knife sharpener.

Cutting requires careful and accurate work. A jagged line or ragged corner will stencil exactly that way in every impression of the stencil plate.

The narrow bridges of paper between the cut-out areas in the design are known as ties. If you accidentally cut through a tie, apply tape to both sides of the tear and replace the tape when needed. Circles and small dots are difficult to cut with a knife. Various large needles can be used to punch out the circles. Ice picks and different-size knitting needles work well. Carefully use the knife or a small piece of fine sandpaper to trim and smooth the edges.

Paints used for stenciling on most surfaces can be water-base or turpentine-base. Any paint used must be mixed to a fairly thick consistency. Acrylic paint is an excellent water-base paint because it is fast drying and easy to clean up. Acrylics are sold in tubes or jars and come in the right consistency for stenciling. Japan paints come in small 8-ounce cans and must be thinned slightly with turpentine. Turpentine-base paints must be allowed to dry for 24 hours. Both acrylic and japan paint dry to a flat finish. As soon as stenciling is completed, brushes are cleaned using water for water-base paints and turpentine for oil- or turpentine-base paints.

When stenciling on paper, use a white or tinted absorbent paper. Metallic or shiny papers should not be utilized unless the stenciling is done with a pen especially perfected for these papers.

Various media can be used for stenciling on paper. Water-base paints, such as acrylics, water-colors or poster paints are especially desirable. Colored pencils can also be used, but the finished project will require spraying with a fixative to prevent smudging. Inks and marking pens—both the permanent and non-permanent varieties—will produce interesting results. Non-permanent inks will require several light coats of a spray fixative. When using marking pens, work quickly to prevent the color from bleeding. A few drops of liquid detergent added to the paint often will make the paint easier to apply, especially on glossy paper. If your paper warps, iron it flat on the reverse side with a cool iron.

Stenciling on fabrics requires textile paints or inks made especially for decorating on fabric. Textile paints and inks come either water- or turpentine-soluble and are mixed thinner than regular paints. The fabric must be prewashed or drycleaned to remove any sizing and allow for shrinkage. Blotters must be used underneath the fabric to absorb excess moisture and paint. After the stenciled fabric has dried, ironing will set the textile paint or ink and make the colors permanent and washable. All these coloring mediums can be purchased at an art-supply store.

Brushes used for stenciling are cylindrical. The bristles are cut all the same length, forming a circular flat surface of bristle ends. Stencil brushes come in various sizes. A good selection of sizes would be ¼ inch in diameter, ½ inch in diameter, and 1 inch in diameter. A clean brush is used each time a new color is introduced. Small strips of household sponge may be used on paper instead of a brush.

Stenciling begins by securing the stencil plate on two sides with masking tape to the object being stenciled. If the plate is not secure, the action of the stencil brush will cause the design to smear. The brush is grasped like a pencil but held perpendicular to the work surface. Dip only the flat bottom of the bristles into the paint. Do not overload the brush with paint, or it will run under the plate and ruin the design. Have several sheets of newspaper nearby for pouncing out the freshly loaded brush. Pouncing is a hammerlike movement that disperses the paint throughout the bristles. When an even speckling of paint is evident on the newspaper, the brush is ready for use. Stippling is the proper term for the rapid up-and-down motion of the brush over the stencil plate. Stippling continues until the openings in the plate are completely filled in with color. When the stenciling has been completed, let the project dry for a few minutes. Then carefully lift up the stencil.

Masking tape is used to keep different colors clean and separate if you desire to use more than one color for a single stencil plate. The varying parts of the design are masked with tape as each color is transferred. Changing the masking tape is done without removing the plate from the project being stenciled.

As soon as stenciling with any plate is finished, the plate is wiped gently with a rag or sponge dampened with water or turpentine depending on the paint in use. This increases the life expectancy of the stencil plate by helping prevent the accumulation of paint around the edges of the design.

Colors can be lightened by the addition of white and grayed and neutralized by the addition of a small amount of the complementary color. Red and green are complements as are blue and orange, yellow and purple. The grayer the color the more faded and aged the final result. Metallic bronzing powders added to paint give the appearance of iridescence. Stencilwork on floors, woodwork and tin should be protected with several coats of good varnish.

A more detailed and specific account of the art of stenciling is contained in *The Complete Book of Stencilcraft* (Simon & Schuster), by Joanne C. Day.

1. CHRISTMAS

2. ST. PATRICK'S DAY

5. HALLOWEEN

6. ST. PATRICK'S DAY

7. BIRTHDAY

8. SHOWER

9. THANKSGIVING

10. THANKSGIVING

13. VALENTINE'S DAY

14. VALENTINE'S DAY

17. BACK TO SCHOOL

18. FOURTH OF JULY

19. FATHER'S DAY

20. FATHER'S DAY OR COLUMBUS DAY

21. VALENTINE'S DAY

22. VALENTINE'S DAY

23. VALENTINE'S DAY

24. BIRTHDAY

25. EASTER

26. EASTER

29. VALENTINE'S DAY

- -

30. MOTHER'S DAY

33. CHRISTMAS

34. CHRISTMAS

37. EASTER

- -

38. EASTER

39. CHRISTMAS

40. CHRISTMAS

41. BIRTHDAY

42. BIRTHDAY

43. MOTHER'S DAY

44. MOTHER'S DAY

45. NEW YEAR'S

46. ST. PATRICK'S DAY

49. CHRISTMAS

50. CHRISTMAS

51. BIRTHDAY OR BABY SHOWER

52. BIRTHDAY

53. CHRISTMAS

54. CHRISTMAS

55. BIRTHDAY

56. WEDDING

57. BABY SHOWER

58. BIRTHDAY

59. CHRISTMAS

60. BIRTHDAY

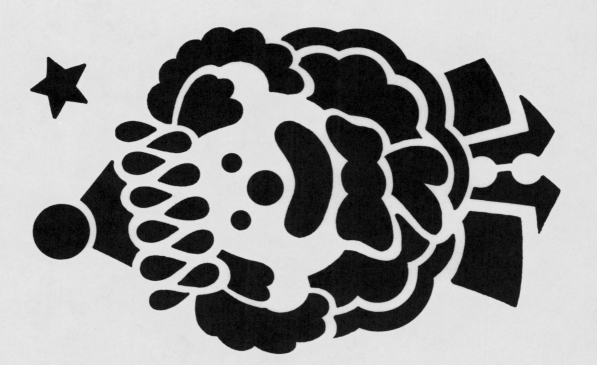